MAX MEETS EMMA

Learning about Blended Families
from a Basset Hound's Perspective

Jennifer Leister, LPC

Illustrations by Raymond Reyes and Ramir Quintana

Dedication

For my loving family—Chris, Emma, and Rhett
For my colleagues—Deirdre and Jennifer

Hi, my name is Max, and I'm a basset hound. I live with Sam, the best boy in the world.

Today Sam and I played with his new ball while he told me some news.

"Christopher is coming over for dinner tonight. Mom says you will have to get a bath before he gets here."

I like baths, so I started to run toward the hose, but Sam said he wasn't ready yet. "You can play with Otis for now. I'll come get you soon."

Otis the Rabbit hopped over as soon as Sam went inside. "Hi, Max. I heard Sam say you're getting a bath."

"Yes, Christopher is coming over for dinner tonight."

"Who's Christopher?" asked Otis.

"Do you remember when Sam's mommy and daddy divorced last year?" I asked Otis.

"Yes," said Otis.

"Christopher is Sam's mommy's boyfriend. They have been dating for a long time now."

"What is dating?" asked Otis.

"Dating is when two grown-ups go to dinner, movies, museums, or dancing," I explained. "Sam told me all about it. Sometimes, grown-ups who are dating fall in love."

"Let's go play, Otis," I said. "All this talking about falling in love is making me feel a little nervous."

9

Later during my bath, Sam told me I had to be on my best behavior. "Mom says that Christopher is bringing Emma to dinner so we can all meet," Sam explained.

"Who's Emma?" I asked.

"Emma is Christopher's cat," Sam answered. "Max, can you play nice tonight?"

"Yes!" I wagged my tail and pretended to be excited, but I really just wanted to scream, "No! SHE'S A CAT!"

When the doorbell rang, I knew Christopher and that cat were here. Sam looked over at me and smiled.

Emma, a black cat with big eyes, strolled in and went straight to my toys and water bowl.

"Look at that, she doesn't even ask to play with my toys!" I thought to myself.

Sam walked over and patted my head. "It's OK, boy, you have to learn to share your toys."

But I didn't want to share my toys and I really didn't want to be friends with a cat!

The next day I played outside with Otis, and I had to tell him all about our visitor.

"Guess what? Christopher came over and brought Emma—his cat. I don't like cats! She didn't want to play catch or tug-of-war or bury anything—not even shoes! And she got mad when I chased her. She's no fun!" I exclaimed.

Otis asked me, "Is Christopher going to marry Sam's mommy?"

"Yes," I sighed. "Sam is happy. He says that Christopher makes his mommy laugh and that he is kind."

"Will Christopher be his new daddy after they marry?" Otis asked.

"No! A stepdad can never replace your dad. Sam said his daddy and mommy are his parents forever," I told Otis. "His new stepdad is a bonus."

I explained to Otis that Christopher is another adult to help with homework and play catch, another adult to love him and take care of him, but Christopher will never replace his daddy.

"Sounds complicated," said Otis.

"Sometimes, human relationships are complicated," I acknowledged. I thought about all the people in Sam's life who loved him—his grandparents, his cousins, aunts and uncles, his parents, and now he would have a new stepfather.

25

The next day when I woke up from my nap, Emma and Christopher were at the house again. I ran outside as fast as I could, but Emma chased me.

"Can I meet your friend Otis?" Emma asked.

"Fine," I told her. "Let's go, but you better keep up! I'm not waiting for a cat!"

Then I ran as fast as I could.

Emma ran pretty fast too though. Who knew cats could move that quickly?

When we met up with Otis, he grinned and said, "Nice to meet you, Emma. Welcome to the neighborhood!"

We played all afternoon. It turned out that Emma was really good at running and jumping.

When Emma left to go home, Otis said, "Max, she's fun, I had no idea a cat could be so much fun."

"I guess so. But why couldn't Christopher have a dog instead?"

Otis shook his head at me before hopping home. I guess a cat was okay to play with—just this once.

Then Emma started coming around a lot. She was really good at chasing me. She could climb up trees and jump down from really high places.

Sometimes, I enjoyed having her chase me, and sometimes I just wanted to rest. But I was starting to get used to her visits.

Then one day, I found a small water and food bowl next to mine and a strange box with sand inside.

Emma told me to keep away from her box.

"Who are you to tell me to keep away from your stuff?" I shouted.

"You better get used to it, buddy," said Emma. "I'm here for good, and I'm not leaving."

Now I was really angry. I forgot about having fun with Emma. All I could think about was how a cat had moved into my house, was drinking my water, and getting attention from my boy, Sam.

This was not good. Not good at all.

"Look," Emma said, "this stinks for me too. I'm used to having my own place. I don't like sharing with a big smelly dog."

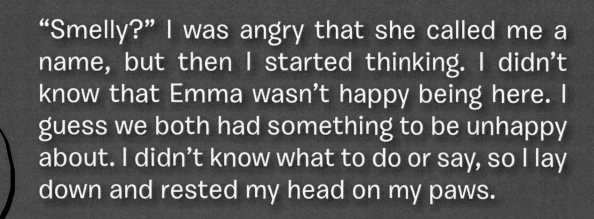

"Smelly?" I was angry that she called me a name, but then I started thinking. I didn't know that Emma wasn't happy being here. I guess we both had something to be unhappy about. I didn't know what to do or say, so I lay down and rested my head on my paws.

Emma lay down too and rested her head on her paws.

Sam came into the room and saw us resting on the floor. Sam got down on his knees and put one hand on my head and one hand on Emma's head.

He told us how he felt about his mommy and Christopher getting married. Sam said he was scared but happy at the same time. He was especially happy that he had both of us, and together we were a new family.

37

I glanced over at Emma. Emma looked back at me. I thought about the fun times I had with Emma. Maybe cats weren't so bad after all.

Emma snuggled next to Sam, and so did I. Then we took a nice, long nap together.

The next day, I told Otis that Sam's mommy was marrying Christopher and that Emma would live with us all the time now.

Otis looked at me. "What do you think about that, Max?"

I thought about all the strange things cats do and how they are so different from dogs and rabbits. But I had to admit, "Emma's not that bad . . . for a cat."

Things were changing. Sometimes, that change is hard. I am learning that sometimes too that change brings good things, like new friends and people who care about you.

38182015R00027

Made in the USA
Middletown, DE
06 March 2019